THE BAKER'S DOZEN
Cookbook Series

Volume 4

# Best Scones

D1567758

Marcy Goldman

RIVER HEART
PRESS

Montreal, Canada

**The Baker's Dozen Series, Volume Four**
**Best Scones**

Text and Recipes by Marcy Goldman

**River Heart Press 2021**
Montreal, Canada

**Library and Archives Canada in Publication**
ISBN 978-1-927936-40-5 Print Book
ISBN 978-1-927936-37-5 E-Book

**Goldman, Marcy**
The Baker's Dozen Series, Volume Four
Marcy Goldman Presents The Baker's Dozen Best Scones

**Other Books by Marcy Goldman**
A Treasury of Jewish Holiday Baking Whitecap Books 2007
The New Best of Betterbaking.com Whitecap Books 2007
When Bakers Cook, River Heart Press 2013
A Passion for Baking, River Heart Press 2014
The Baker's Four Seasons River Heart Press 2014
Love and Ordinary Things River Heart Press 2014
The Newish Jewish Cookbook River Heart Press 2019

**Marcy Goldman's The Baker's Dozen Series** River Heart Press
The Baker's Dozen Volume One Best Holiday Cookies 2016
The Baker's Dozen Volume Two Best Biscotti 2017
The Baker's Dozen Volume Three Best Bagels 2018
The Baker's Dozen Volume Four Best Scones 2021

# Table of Contents

## Introduction – All About Scones

## Recipes

# The Baker's Dozen Cookbook Series
## Volume 4
# Best Scones

## Introduction
## Welcome to the beautiful world of Scones!

If you visit your local café these days you're likely to find a pretty decent selection of scones vying with the usual muffins and biscotti. This is relatively recent because back in the day, at least in North America, you couldn't find a scone for love or money. Happily in the last several years, a lot has changed and now scones are a familiar sight in sandwich shops and bakeries as well as your favorite café. Scones also may be undisputedly British in heritage but seeing the wonderful varieties on this side of the pond is a true testimony to the baking creativity on this side of the pond.

As innovative, imaginative bakers tend to do, we've taken the roots of this pastry into a whole new and inventive realm. As a professional baker I love fiddling with scones! In this very special collection in this cookbook, I've tried to retain what I like about scones, i.e. their pastry like flakiness but still keep them…. well, still scones. From this starting point, I've played with a host of variations and approaches that, at least to my mind, only make scones even more exciting and tasty. More than that, I've included some hallmark baker's secret tips and techniques to make your scones stellar!

## A little scone history

Scones are believed to have originated in Scotland (as well as England and Wales) where they were made with oats, shaped in a large round, scored in triangles and cooked on a stone griddle or open fire. The Scots' claim to scones is largely because of scones may well have originated in Scotland and this is often attributed to the first known print reference of scones, in 1513, is from a Scottish poet. Scones also very closely resemble Irish soda bread and both are closely related to the griddle-baked flatbread known as bannock we know in North America. From scones came baking powder biscuits, with which most of us are familiar. Baking a simple dough in a fireplace or on a stove top griddle or cast iron pan probably goes back centuries when people would slap together simple doughs to make a quick bread. It just seems the British Isles, then the colonies, really adopted them. Scones became more refined as well as popular when they became part of afternoon tea in England. According to many sources, Anna, the seventh Dutchess of Bedford (1788-1861) is credited with making scones into a culinary fashion trend. *"It was in 1840 she felt a sinking feeling around mid-afternoon so she ordered the servants to bring some tea and sweet breads, including scones'* to nibble on. I imagine that is the first official recording of someone being 'peckish'. "She was so delighted by this that she ordered it every afternoon in what became the English tradition of afternoon tea time (precisely 4 pm) or high tea. Scones are still served daily with the traditional, clotted cream topping in Britain and around the world'. (Source for quote www.worldfoodhistory.com)

Scones have greatly evolved since the invention of modern day baking powder in the 1860's. Nothing gave scones (as well as biscuits, cakes, cookies) more lift and rise, if you pardon the pun, than the luxury of reliable baking powder. Before then, baking soda or, pearl ash and sourdough starters had been the rising agent and results of baked goods could be a bit wonky. Scones might have been good enough before modern baking powder cane into being but since *that* invention, given a good recipe and technique to begin with, they've been spectacular!

Scones can be rather glamorous but for all intent and purposes, they are essentially simple biscuits but they are more often wedge-shaped (than round) and are plumper, sweeter and overall, more beautiful. This is why they are an ideal treat to pair with tea or coffee.

Scones call exclusively for butter (never shortening or margarine) and pantry basics like sugar, eggs and flour. But after that they can be decked out with a myriad of good things, mostly sweet or nutty but sometimes savory (as in my favorite *Rustic Cheddar Cheese Scone*) before being cut into wedges (or dropped) and baked. The possibilities are virtually endless!

What I love about scones is their flakiness and simplicity of taste; there's nothing too ooey-gooey here! Since they're not overtly decadent scones never make you feel like you've over-indulged. A good scone goes a long way in creating an oasis of relaxation. One eats a scone leisurely so that you can enjoy each bite and that only prolongs the pleasure.

## Quick and Easy Scones

What I like best about scones however is that they are incredibly fast and easy, making them my first thought when hosting an impromptu visit from a friend. This is also something to consider because since scones, unless eaten or frozen for later, can be less than optimal a day later. By implication that means the best and freshest have to be homemade. Everywhere else scones are served, you can run into really dry scones so home bakers have such an edge here.

# Scone Technique Basics

## Ingredients

Scones are simply scrambled together from the bakery essentials of milk or buttermilk, butter, eggs (although not always), sugar, salt, and baking powder. What's really crucial about scones is how you cut in the butter as well as the freshness of the baking powder. Other add-in's such as pure vanilla extract or other flavor extracts, chocolate chips, citrus zest, nuts and cheese are what dramatically changes the flavor or even texture of a scone. So be sure to use the best and handle all ingredients with care.

## Sugar

Most of the time, my recipes call for white sugar. When brown sugar is called for, it is golden or light brown sugar. You can swap sugar alternates and experiment but these recipes were tested with traditional sugar as the sweetener of record.

## Pure Vanilla Extract and Other Extracts

Vanilla is another core ingredient and a default flavor note in so much baking. I always use pure vanilla extract and most often, I choose the **Nielsen Massey** brand available in some supermarkets, gourmet stores or you can order it online. What you want in vanilla is its purity, but also a warm, resounding, full flavor. Pure vanilla, like true love, changes everything for the good. If you can't find Nielsen Massey, try Costco or McCormicks brand.

## Orange Oil, Lemon Oil

Boyajian is a leading citrus oil company offering all natural, intense citrus oils. If you use these, use half as much as you would use orange or lemon extract.

## Almond, Orange, Lemon, Extracts

McCormicks, as well as Nielsen Massey and Boyijian and some other companies, offers wonderful, pure extracts that as much as fresh orange juice, or lemon zest, or toasted almonds, offer yet another flavor dimension to baked goods. Use the best and purest extracts ones you can find. I often combine extracts in a recipe, perhaps vanilla with orange for a unique, uplifted taste.

## Flour, White, Unbleached All-Purpose

When choosing be aware there are a few types of all-purpose flour or any flour for that matter, loosely divided into bleached (the regular supermarket flour that is most common), unbleached (naturally aged) and organic.

Find an all-purpose flour that you prefer and that performs as per your expectations and for the most part, until you choose to venture into another brand, stay with the same flour in order to expect consistent results and get familiar with how a flour behaves in recipes. For this cookbook as with most of my cookbooks and recipe testing, I rely on an unbleached, all-purpose flour, such as Robin Hood or Five Roses. In the States, there are many brands such as King Arthur Flour, Pillsbury and Gold Medal.

## Flour, Whole-Wheat

Here you have a choice between stone-ground or regular whole-wheat flour, as well as white whole-wheat. I prefer stone-ground whole wheat because it features all the great components of 'whole' wheat –the full wheat berry. Often, supermarket whole-wheat is simply white enriched flour with traces of bran added to it. In the industry, they call this 'restored' whole wheat meaning they strip it of lots of its goodness and then 'restore' the bran back. It is a for-show sort of whole-wheat, i.e. it's only 'whole' wheat in name. So it's always better to go with stone-ground, either a regular stone-ground or an organic variety. White whole-wheat flour is also a whole-wheat flour but it's a bit sweeter (there's no characteristic bitterness some whole-wheat flour can have) and perfect for scone making.

When I measure flour I whisk or stir it a bit in its canister, then simply scoop, using a metal dry measure cup, and level off the top.

## White Sugar

White sugar, also known as granulated sugar is the basic sweetener in most of the recipes in this book. Occasionally, some recipes call for extra fine white sugar. That is simply white sugar, pulverized a bit finer in a food processor. To measure white sugar, just scoop it using a metal measuring cup. Do not use a glass or liquid measuring cup for dry ingredients such as sugar because it does not always measure the same.

## Brown Sugar, Light, Golden and Dark

Brown sugar is generally a sugar with traces of molasses in it. It offers a special flavor and slight caramel kiss to your baking, and a certain warm, sweet taste. It can be used alone in some recipes or in conjunction with white sugar in many others. Brown sugar, when called for, is usually golden or light brown but dark will work if you are out of light or golden brown sugar. To measure brown sugar, regardless if it is lighter or darker hue, scoop the sugar into the metal measuring cup and lightly pat down. This is what is known firmly packed. Since it is a moist sugar and is less fine than white sugar, packing it down ensures that you have enough sugar or at least, an accurate measure of this sugar.

## Confectioners' Sugar or Icing Sugar

Confectioners' sugar or icing sugar, as it is called in Canada, is a white sugar pulverized with cornstarch. It is used in butter-based icings or for dusting on top of cakes and pastries as a finishing touch. It also can be mixed with a tiny bit of extracts, food coloring, butter, and/or liquid (water, juice, coffee – as per the recipe) if you are using it to make a quick glaze or fondant (the white drippy stuff you see on donuts and supermarket coffeecakes). You can use this quickly made fondant to dip a cupcake into or to drizzle on a yeasted pastry or to glitz up cinnamon buns. On the other hand, if you are able to procure baker's soft fondant, use that. It tastes better than quick fondant.

Another tip? If you're whipping heavy cream, use confectioners' sugar in it instead of regular white sugar to make a more stable whipping cream.

## Butter, Unsalted or Sweet Butter

Great baking depends on a balance of structure (flour and eggs and leaveners), sweetness (sugar, etc.) and fat, which is an integral part of a recipe's flavor, texture, taste, and conservation. I use unsalted or sweet butter in 90% of my baking. Butter is usually creamed with sugar as a basic step in cakes or cookies for example. This imports air and lightness in a recipe. But in scones, the butter in cut in, as you do for pie pastry. Just remember, that nothing tastes or performs like butter. It is that simple. Even in country biscuits, where recipes can call for shortening – I use butter.

When you find unsalted butter on sale, stock up! A block of butter freezes well for a few months and is fine in the refrigerator for 2-3 weeks. Butter is measured is in cups for my recipes (not by sticks or by weight).

1 pound butter = 2 cups
1/2 pound butter = 1 cup
1/4 pound butter = 1/2 cup
1/8 pound butter = 14 cup

Very cold butter is best for best in scones and other pastries. You can even freeze cubes of butter you intend to use in your scones.

## Eggs

Eggs provide flavor, color, leavening, and tenderness and are part of the structure in any baked goods. In scones, eggs also provide some structure, and they also add to preservation, keeping the scone fresh a little longer.

All recipes in this book call for large eggs. Results will not be the same using extra-large, jumbo, or medium. Brown or white eggs are both fine. But *all* types of baking profits from using room temperature eggs. Take them out about an hour before baking or douse them in hot water in a bowl, for 2 minutes before cracking them opening and using in a recipe. The volume or loft in your scones will be noticeable.

## Milk

Whole milk is a regular companion in the baker's kitchen. You can use any fat milk, 1%, 2% or 3.5% without a discernable difference in flavor but do know, that milk, a dairy product, assists with browning (and flavor) in baked goods. Milk is best used a room temperature in baking recipes. Milk also introduces tenderness in baked goods, and as all liquids in baking, greatly expands the crumb of a cake, scone or cookie.

## Cream

The recipes here use light cream or half-and-half or sometimes, whipping cream (which is generally identifiable on the carton, whipping cream and usually contains 35% fat). Cream, because of its added fat content, tenderizes things even more than milk does. It is ideal in scones! If a recipe calls for light cream or half-and-half, you can use that or 12%, 15%, and 18% pretty interchangeably and swapping in whipping cream if that is what you have on hand is fine.

Incidentally if you have a lot of cream on hand and the recipe calls for buttermilk, just add a teaspoon of lemon juice per cup of cream to replicate the buttermilk called for. That said, soured cream (cream and lemon juice) make the most tender and flakey scones possible! It's become my new way of making all my scones lately.

## Buttermilk, Sour Milk, Sour Cream Yogurt and Buttermilk Powder

Buttermilk is one of the nicest additions to any baking and it figures in many of my recipes. Back in the farm days, buttermilk was often used in baking as it was plentiful and it only helped showcase great baking even more due to the attributes and benefits of buttermilk in everyday baking.

Buttermilk is a velvety dairy liquid and while it is now made as it used to be buttermilk being the resultant liquid when you churned butter; now it is skim milk, with a bacterial culture introduced to sour it. It offers acidity, the better to interact with baking soda in recipes, which in turn aids in leavening, a subtle but tasty tang, vitamins and calcium. The only drawback is that unless you bake with it or drink it regularly, you might not always have it on hand. In this case you can use sour milk: one cup of milk mixed with a tablespoon of lemon juice or vinegar. You can also swap in loose plain yogurt.

## Buttermilk Powder

Another buttermilk trick is to have a back-up of buttermilk powder, a pantry ready product you can get in bulk food stores or from **Saco Foods**. Saco Foods offers an all-natural pure Buttermilk Blend, a dry, natural buttermilk powder that is a superb substitute in any recipes that call for real, fresh buttermilk. In addition to Saco Foods, I recommend Hoosier Farms Buttermilk Powder which you can get via the company itself or on Amazon.

When you *do* use buttermilk powder remember the buttermilk powder goes in with the flour and substitute water for the liquid. The exact conversion is four tablespoons buttermilk powder and 1 cup water to replace one cup of real buttermilk.

Sour cream and yogurt are pretty much interchangeable although sour cream offers far more fat (unless it is low or no fat) than the standard yogurt. Yogurt and buttermilk are interchangeable, both similar in fat content and in how loose they are (versus sour cream which is considerably thicker). All three are acidic dairy products that perform in similar ways, offer that subtle but characteristic tang and help with leavening.

## Leaveners

There are several ways to get your baked goods raised. There is: steam, air, chemicals (soda and powder), gas (yeast into carbon dioxide, whether it's commercial dry yeast or airborne yeast spores), and eggs (which provide expansion as well as structure in a recipe). Some recipes use one or another or a combinations of leaveners but scones are most often made with baking powder and/or baking soda.

## Baking Powder

The best advice about baking powder is that the best powder is that it should be as fresh as can be. Baking powder is essentially a mixture of baking soda, mixed with an acid and some cornstarch as a carrier. Once baking powder is in a batter and is moistened, its action (leavening) begins. Continuous, or the 'second action' (hence the term double acting) action continues with the heat of the oven.

To ascertain whether baking powder is fresh, mix a teaspoonful of powder with a half-cup of warm water and 1 teaspoon lemon juice. The mixture should bubble and foam. If not, it is no longer viable or active and it is best to buy a new can. All recipes here were tested with Clabber Girl, Davis Brand and in Canada, Magic Baking powder. Baking powder, unopened, usually has a 6-month 'best before' date. Once opened, it is optimal for about 3 months. So always make sure your baking powder is absolutely fresh and at top performance. If you have any doubt, invest in a new can!

## Baking Soda

Unlike baking powder, which is a combination of cornstarch, soda and an acid, baking soda is simply soda. It is called for when there is more than the usual acid in a recipe (buttermilk, for example) than the baking powder, alone, can neutralize. In such case, some recipes only rely on baking soda (many soda breads, some cookies), and some use less, in ratio to some baking powder also called for. Baking soda does not have a past due date; it has no expiry. If you taste a soapy or off taste in baking, chances are, you have used too much baking soda. Do not use the baking soda you use to keep your fridge smelling fresh in your baked goods! It is like an absorbent sponge and will negatively affect the taste of the finished baked goods.

## Salt

Salt is used in sweet baking as well as all baking as a counterbalance the sweetness in a recipe and make the flavors sing. Salt is the little black dress of baking in how essential and effective it is. It is the most overlooked ingredient and yet too much or too little vastly affects a recipe. If you can, find fine kosher salt at kosher websites such as www.koshermart.com or in supermarkets). Kosher salt is an iodine-free, lightly salty, and pure salt, which is ideal for baking. Regular salt is saltier and has a telltale taste of iodine. Sea salt is a good swap for kosher salt.

## Chocolate

Dark chocolate is also called semi-sweet or bittersweet. They have different percentages of ground pure chocolate in them but are interchangeable for the most part. Different companies also term the same chocolate differently than from their competitors but optimally, it is about percentages of chocolate in them.

Dark, semi-sweet or bittersweet chocolate is the most common chocolates used in baking. Unsweetened used to be used a fair amount but is out of vogue. It is pure chocolate without any added sugar or vanilla.

Milk chocolate has less chocolate liqueur, as well as sugar, milk and vanilla added to it. White chocolate has only cocoa fat in it; no chocolate liqueur in it, as well as sugar and milk. It is called white chocolate but it is actually, its own unique confection and is a great boost in so many recipes and simply sounds, (as well as tastes), divine. Finding the best chocolate you can afford is the best advice for chocolate. It shines through all your baking. I recommend Callebaut, Valrohna and Toblerone and Lindt among other imported brands or in American, Scharffen Berger Chocolate is outstanding.

Chocolate chips, whether they are milk, dark or white chocolate, should be *real* chocolate. Make sure when you pick up a package that says so, and not *'chocolate flavored'* chips. Instead of chips, you are also use chopped up chocolate as a change in baking, upgrading a typical chocolate chip cookie.

Other brands and formats such as Nestles, Chipits, Hershey's, Baker's and the quality supermarket brands do an admirable job whenever chocolate chips, semi-sweet or milk, are called for.

For white chocolate in particular, which is so tricky to melt, Callebaut, Lindt, and Valrona are recommended brands. White chocolate discs from confectionary supply places may melt easily but have no taste and are not really chocolate. If white chocolate is not really chocolate, white chocolate 'wafers' are beyond six degrees of separation.

Melt chocolate slowly in a bowl in the microwave (20-30 seconds at a time at low power or in a double boiler over the lowest possible heat. Slow and steady makes for properly melted chocolate, especially in the case of white chocolate, which can be quite a primadonna. Stir to cool it before adding it to recipes lest it melt the butter or cook the eggs in the recipe. For melting all chocolate, make sure no water or steam comes into contact with the chocolate or it will seize up.

## Cocoa

Cocoa is a pure chocolate product that has no milk, sugar, vanilla added to it nor does it contain any cocoa fat. It is about the consistency of cornstarch. It makes little difference whether you use cocoa with alkali treatment in it (otherwise known as Dutched or Dutch Process) or untreated, non-Dutch cocoa although Dutch cocoa generally produces darker hued chocolate cakes and other things and some purport (I do) a more subtle but distinct, defined, pure chocolate taste when using Dutch process cocoa.

Measure cocoa by stirring it only slightly in its container to break up any big lumps, scooping and measuring by scraping off. Generally, add it to the dry ingredients of a recipe, whisking with a hand whisk to blend it into the flour and leaveners.

## Nuts, Dried Fruit

As with all things but particularly with nuts, taste before you use them. Fatty and natural, nuts can turn rancid before they ever arrive in your pantry for baking. Store nuts in the freezer to keep longer. Toast nuts lightly for best flavor.

Dried fruit varies in quality but for the most part, whether it's dried cherries, raisins, dried cranberries, or apricots, all dried fruit profits from plumping by being covered by boiling water for several minutes. Then drain and pat dry with paper towels and then and proceed to the fruit to the recipe when called for. In all my recipes, the term, *plumped and dried,* (e.g. 1 cup raisins, plumped and dried) means to cover with very hot water for a few minutes, then drain, dry with paper towels and use.

## Spices

Nothing contravenes great baking quite as effectively as using bland, stale or poor quality spices. There are many places to find specialty spices online or exploring your own city so really demand the best. **Never** assume that all cinnamon, cloves, or allspice are equal. Invest in fragrant and vibrant fresh spices (and in small amounts). Taste or smell them before tossing them into your scone recipe. The difference in using superlative spices is remarkable. Sourcing them out is also a wonderful baker's adventure.

I most often turn to Penzeys, The Spice House, Silk Road Spices (in Canada) and I've never been disappointed with a fresh container of Costco's cinnamon. But spices are the hallmark extra grace note in baking so give them the care they deserve. Your baking will thank you for it.

# Danish Dough Whisk

## Techniques

### Mixing and Handling Scones

Aside from simple but great quality ingredients scones are totally dependent on how you cut the fat into the flour. Like pie dough, scones are about three things: technique, technique and technique! Tender, artful handling is where the flakiness of scones begins its journey.

As with pie dough, cold butter and cold liquids will result in the best-textured scones. Make sure that the butter comes straight from the fridge and the liquid ingredients are as icy cold as possible. Some bakers actually freeze the cubes of butter beforehand.

Almost any first step in any scone recipe instructs you to cut in or rub in the butter. What this means is to cut up or cut in the butter into small bits into the flour until it resembles coarse meal or a sandy, grainy flour. This can be done by gently sanding the flour and butter between your finger-tips or by using two knives, cutting through the butter and flour in a motion that resembles cutting meat into small bits on a plate. The resulting flour-coated little grains are then just moistened with the liquid ingredient until they barely cohere. Then you add in the eggs, liquids, and other ingredients such as dried fruit, nuts or chocolate. You can also do this step in a food processor, pulsing gently to break the fat into the butter. At that point, I dump the mixture into a bowl and continue by hand.

It's a good idea to always hold back some of the liquid, i.e. buttermilk, milk or cream, rather than dump it all in at once. Depending on climatic or ingredient idiosyncrasies you may need less than more liquid. Once the grains are moistened, stir the dough with your hand in the bowl into a shaggy mass.

Turn rough mass of dough out onto a lightly floured board and gently knead; no more than 8-10 kneads or 10-12 seconds worth. Do not overwork it until it is too smooth. The heat of your hands will begin to warm the butter and the gluten content of the flour will likely be provoked.

Use a cookie cutter dipped in flour to cut round scones and make the cut in one clean motion. Do not twist as you remove the cookie cutter as this tends to lock the flaky layers together or results in having the scone topple sideways in the oven during baking.

## Cutting and/or Shape of Scones

You can cut your scones in wedges or in circles. You can also cut large circles and then cut those in half to achieve a wedge! You can also use a regular or mini scone pan. My scone pans are from Nordicware available from the company online or via Amazon. I find them irreplaceable for making perfect, uniform scones, especially nice if you are making scones for a party such as a bridal shower or as a Thanksgiving side bread or for giving them as gifts. Free-form scones bake up more flakey and crust, especially around their edges but pan-formed scones are regular and there's less guess-work in achieving size and weight regularity. You can also use the scone pans for making perfect holiday cornbread wedges.

# Nordicware Scone Pan

## Baking

I've tested many temperatures for these scone recipes and the best method is:

**Double-stack to baking sheets together and line the top one with parchment paper.**

**Bake on middle rack of oven.**

**Bake all scones unless otherwise stated at 400 F°.**

## Storage

Scones freeze well, stored in a Ziploc bag and then frozen. You can also mix the dry ingredients for any scone recipe and freeze that. Then take it out of the freezer and finish the recipe.

To store or gift fresh scones, wrap each one in wax paper and then put them in a pastry box or tin. They last 1-2 days for gifting.

## Best Classic Buttermilk Scones

# Best Classic Buttermilk Scones

*The generous measure of butter in these scones goes a long way in making them especially flaky and rich. Since butter is the star ingredient shop around for better ones, experimenting with imported Irish or European butters or local organic ones. This is a great basic, rich scone that you can add almost anything to but they are wonderful just pure and simple.*

4 cups all-purpose flour
½ cup sugar
½ teaspoon salt
2 teaspoons baking powder
½ teaspoon baking soda
1 ½ cups unsalted butter, in small cubes
1 ¼ cups buttermilk
1 ½ teaspoons pure vanilla extract
1 egg
1 cup blueberries, optional

Preheat oven to 400° F. Stack two baking sheets together and line the top one with parchment paper. Arrange the oven rack to the upper third position.

In a food processor bowl, add the flour, sugar, salt, baking powder, baking soda and blend ingredients briefly. Cut in the butter to make a coarse, grainy mixture. Turn out into a large bowl. Make a well in the center add most of the buttermilk, vanilla and the egg, stir lightly with a fork to blend and bring into a mass that holds together somewhat.

Turn out onto a lightly floured board and knead 8-10 times, until mixture is just barely rollable adding in a little more flour if dough seems too soft or isn't holding together. Add in blueberries if using. Pat or roll out 1 inch thick and cut into 3 ½ - 4inch rounds with a cookie cutter. Cut in half again to form wedges with a cookie cutter. To do this, you cut a circle of 4 inches and then cut it in half - this will give you nice wedges. Brush tops with melted butter or sweet milk, dust with sugar and bake until golden, about 12-15 minutes.

***Makes 8-12 scones***

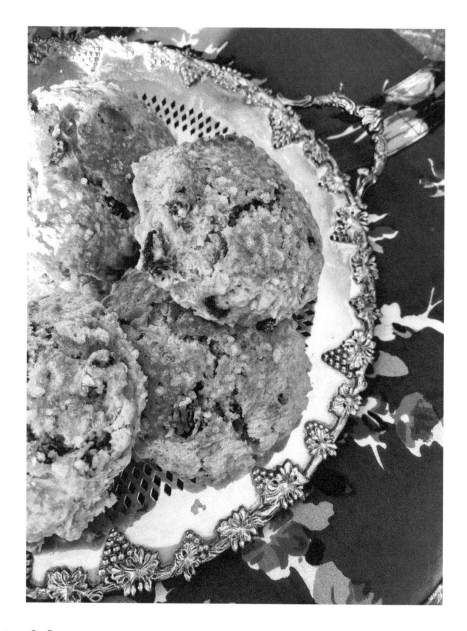

**Bridgerton's Golden Oatmeal Scones**

# Bridgerton's Golden Oatmeal Scones

*Nothing beats these very British scones with their touch of rustic whole-wheat flour and nutty oatmeal. Add a touch of spice, currants or raisins, a lashing of buttermilk and you have beautifully classic, Bridgerton-style scones for your next high tea.*

## Scones

½ cup oatmeal
2 2/3 cup all-purpose flour
2/3 cup whole-wheat flour
1/3 cup brown sugar, firmly packed
5 tablespoons white sugar
3/4 teaspoon salt
2 teaspoons baking powder
1 teaspoon baking soda
¼ teaspoon cloves
1 teaspoon cinnamon
¾ cup unsalted butter, in small cubes
1 egg
1- 1 1/4 cup buttermilk or whipping cream
½ cup currants, plumped
½ cup raisins, plumped

## Finishing Touches

Milk, cream, or melted unsalted butter
Demerara, coarse or regular sugar

Preheat the oven to 400° F. Stack a large baking sheet on top of another one and line the top one with parchment paper. Arrange the oven rack to the middle or upper third position.

In a food processor add in the oatmeal, flour, wheat flour, brown sugar, white sugar, salt, baking powder, baking soda, cloves and cinnamon and blend ingredients briefly. Add in the butter and pulse to create a mealy or coarse mixture. Turn the mixture out into a large bowl. Make a well in the center and add the egg and most of the buttermilk. Mix with a fork to make a stiff dough, add gently mix in the currants and raisins. Turn out onto a lightly floured board and knead 8-10 times, until mixture is just barely rollable adding in a little more flour if dough seems too soft or isn't holding together.

Roll or press out to at thickness of 1-inch. Using a plain or fluted 3-inch cutter, cut into rounds. Brush with melted butter and dust with the sugar of your choice.

Bake until lightly browned around the edges, 20-22 minutes.

***Makes 15-20 small scones***

**Cinnamon Bun Scones**

# Cinnamon Bun Scones

*These beautiful scones feature that wonderful taste of a traditional yeasted cinnamon bun but without the fuss. These scones sport a sweet cinnamon outer coating that hides a tender inner scone crumb.*

## Scones

3 cups all-purpose flour
3/8 teaspoon salt
4 teaspoons baking powder
1 cup sugar
3/4 cup unsalted butter, in small cubes
2 teaspoons pure vanilla extract
2 eggs
1 cup whipping cream

## Cinnamon Dip

4 tablespoons unsalted butter, melted
2 teaspoons cinnamon
2-3 cups confectioners' sugar
4-6 t tablespoons whipping cream or milk

Preheat the oven to 400° F. Stack two baking sheets together and line the top one with parchment paper. Arrange the oven rack to the upper third position.

In a food processor, add the flour, salt, baking powder and sugar and blend briefly. Add in the butter and pulse to break it into the dry ingredients to make a coarse, grainy mixture.

Turn out into a large bowl. Make a well in the center and stir in the vanilla, eggs and whipping cream to make a soft dough. If it's very stiff, add more liquid.

Using a small ice-cream scoop, deposit 15-20 scones on the baking sheet.

Bake, 22-25 minutes or until scones are puffy and golden brown. As scones cool, prepare the Cinnamon Dip. For the Cinnamon Dip, whisk together all ingredients until you have a thick, but drippy glaze. Add in more confectioners' sugar or milk/cream as required. Dip scones once, then a second time to set, in Cinnamon Dip.

***Makes 15-20 small scones***

# Sweet Raspberry Ricotta Scones

# Sweet Raspberry Ricotta Scones

*These are my newest, favorite scones since they're the last ones to be tested for this cookbook. You can't beat fresh raspberries, nestled in a ricotta-rich batter baked up to a buttery crisp crust. These are stunning in taste and looks.*

## Scones

2 ½ cups all-purpose flour
3/8 teaspoon salt
1 tablespoon baking powder
½ teaspoon baking soda
1/3 cup sugar
2 teaspoons fresh lemon zest
½ cup unsalted butter, in small cubes
¾ - 1 cup light cream
1 ½ teaspoons pure vanilla extract
1 egg
3/4 cup whole milk ricotta
1 cup fresh raspberries

## Finishing Touches

Milk or cream
Sugar

Preheat oven to 400° F. Stack two baking sheets together and line the top one with parchment paper. Arrange the oven rack to the upper third position.

In a food processor bowl, blend together flour, salt, baking powder, baking soda, sugar and lemon zest. Add the butter into the mixture with fingertips or pastry cutter, or if using a food processor, pulse butter in to make a grainy mixture. Turn mixture out into a large bowl.

Add most of the cream, vanilla, egg and ricotta and stir to form a soft dough before gently folding in the raspberries. Carefully knead dough into an even mass a few minutes adding in a bit more flour if it is too sticky or a little more cream if it is too stiff.

Transfer the dough to a well-floured counter, flour the top of the dough and pat it into a 7-inch round about 1-inch tall. With a 3 ½ inch cookie cutter, cut into 4-5 circles.

Place scones on baking sheet. Brush with cream and sprinkle on sugar.

Bake 15-20 minutes or until lightly golden at the edges. Cool in pan for a minute and then transfer to a cooling rack.

***Makes 8-9 scones***

## Rustic Double Cheddar Scones

# Rustic Double Cheddar Scones

*These are hunky, cheesy scones that are flakey with pastry-goodness and stuffed with cheddar-filled crevices. This is a scone that is a perfect foundation for a breakfast sandwich or alongside a basket of Southern fried chicken.*

## Scones

1 cup strong cheddar cheese, in ½ inch chunks
½ cup shredded strong cheddar cheese
2 – 2 ¼ cups all-purpose flour
¾ teaspoon salt
2 teaspoons sugar
1 teaspoon dry mustard
¼ teaspoon cayenne
4 ½ teaspoons baking powder
½ teaspoon baking soda
½ cup unsalted butter, in small cubes
1 egg
1 cup buttermilk

## Finishing Touches

½ cup melted butter

Preheat the oven to 400° F. Stack two baking sheets together and line the top one with parchment paper. Arrange the oven rack to the upper third position.

Prepare the cheddar in chunks and shred the half-cup shredded. Set aside.

In food processor bowl, blend the flour, salt, sugar, mustard, cayenne, baking powder and baking soda. Break in the butter to make a coarse grainy mixture. Fold in the cheddar chunks and shredded cheddar and turn the mixture out into a large bowl. Make a well in the center and stir in the egg and buttermilk; mix to make a rough dough that forms a mass.

Turn the dough out onto a lightly floured work surface and knead slightly to make dough you can pat out into 1 inch thick. Cut in wedges 8-10 wedges.

Place scones on the baking sheet and brush with some butter.

Bake until golden brown, about 17-20 minutes. Brush again with butter.

***Makes 8-10 scones***

# Blueberry Blackberry Honey Butter Dipped Scones

# Blueberry Blackberry Honey Butter Dipped Scones

*Brush these wonderful scones with warm honey butter as they come out of the oven. It ensures that the scones stay wonderfully flavorful for a few days and the sweetened crust is irresistible. Almost any fruit would do in these, but the mix of blueberries and blackberries is exceptional.*

## Scones

1 – 1 ¼ cup whipping cream
1 tablespoon fresh lemon juice
3 cups all-purpose flour
3/8 teaspoon salt
2/3 cup sugar
4 teaspoons baking powder
½ teaspoon baking soda
¾ cup unsalted butter, in small cubes
1 egg
2 teaspoons pure vanilla extract
½ cup frozen blueberries
¾ cup frozen blackberries
Milk or melted butter

## Honey Glaze

¼ cup unsalted butter, melted
1/3 cup honey

Put the lemon juice in a 1-cup measuring cup and pour in whipping cream to the 1-cup mark.

Preheat the oven to 400° F. Stack a large baking sheet on top of another one and line the top one with parchment paper. Arrange the oven rack to the middle or upper third position.

In a food processor, blend the flour, salt, sugar, baking powder and baking soda briefly. Add in butter and pulse to break up butter into dry ingredients. Turn out into a large bowl. Make a well in the center. Add in egg, vanilla and most of the cream (which will be clotted looking; that is fine). Stir, adding in a touch more flour if required until mixture holds together and makes soft but firm dough. Gently add in the berries. Press out onto a lightly floured work surface to a diameter of one inch. Cut into 8-10 wedges or rounds and place on the baking sheet. Brush each scone with melted butter or milk. Bake 16-19 minutes, until scones are nicely browned.

For the Honey Glaze, heat honey and butter in a measuring cup in the microwave until mixture is just simmering and stir well.

Brush scones once, lightly, as they come out of oven. Let stand on baking sheet. Repeat with some more Honey Butter glaze, more generously, about 15 minutes later.

***Makes about 8-10 scones***

**Pumpkin Pie Latte Scones**

# Pumpkin Pie Latte Scones

*These are autumnal scones with a sweet and pretty glaze that are redolent with fragrant pumpkin pie spice. They're perfect for fall but just as welcome anytime.*

## Scones

2 3/4 cups all-purpose flour

3/4 cup white sugar

1/3 cup brown sugar, firmly packed

¼ teaspoon salt

1/4 teaspoon baking soda

2 1/2 teaspoons baking powder

2 teaspoons pumpkin pie spice

¼ teaspoon cloves

1 ½ teaspoon cinnamon

1/2 cup unsalted butter, in small cubes

1 egg

1 cup canned pure pumpkin puree

1 teaspoon pure vanilla extract

½ - 3/4 cup buttermilk

Milk

## Pumpkin Pie Latte Glaze

4 ounces cream cheese, softened

1 tablespoon unsalted butter

½ teaspoon pure vanilla extract

¼ teaspoon orange oil, optional

1 cup confectioners' sugar

Cream

Orange zest

Preheat oven to 400° F. Stack two baking sheets together and line the top one with parchment paper. Arrange the oven rack to the upper third position.

In a food processor bowl, add the flour, white sugar, brown sugar, salt, baking soda, baking powder, pumpkin pie spice, cinnamon and cloves and blend briefly. Add in the butter and pulse to make a coarse, grainy mixture. Turn the mixture out into a large bowl. Make a well in the center and add egg, pumpkin puree, vanilla, and most of buttermilk. Stir to make a soft dough; if the mixture seems dry, drizzle in a bit more buttermilk.

Turn dough out onto a lightly floured board. Knead a few times to make a smooth mass. Divide dough in two portions and flatten into rounds, about 1 inch thick.

Cut in six wedges each. Brush tops with a little milk and bake until lightly golden brown on top, about 18-20 minutes.

Meanwhile, in a small bowl, blend cream cheese, butter, vanilla, orange oil and confectioners' sugar to make a spreadable glaze, adding in some cream to achieve the right consistency. Spread some glaze on each cooled scone and garnish with orange zest.

***Makes 12 small scones***

**New England Cranberry Orange Scones**

# New England Cranberry Orange Scones

*There's so many cranberry scone recipes and yet each one is different. This one makes an exceptional tender and flaky scone. This is also a recipe that you can make in miniatures and serve at a bridal tea.*

## Scones

1 1/2 cups coarsely chopped frozen cranberries
3 cups all-purpose flour
Zest of one orange, finely minced
2/3 cup sugar
3/8 teaspoon salt
1 tablespoon baking powder
3/4 cup unsalted butter, in small cubes
2 eggs
1 ½ teaspoons pure vanilla extract
1/3 - 1/2 cup whipping cream or more, as required

## Topping

Whipping cream
Sugar

Preheat the oven to 400° F. Stack a large baking sheet on top of another one and line the top one with parchment paper. Arrange the oven rack to the middle or upper third position.

In a food processor, coarsely chop the cranberries and set aside. In a food processor bowl, blend the flour, orange zest, sugar, salt and baking powder in a large bowl or food processor and pulse briefly to blend. Add in the butter and cut in or pulse until mixture is mealy. Turn the mixture out into a large bowl. Make a well in the center and stir in eggs, vanilla and cream to make a soft but firm dough. Fold in cranberries. Knead by hand briefly on a floured work surface and then pat into a large round on a floured surface. Dough should be about 1 inch thick. Cut into 4-inch circles, and then cut these in half. Brush generously with cream and sprinkle on sugar.

Bake for 15-20 minutes.

***Makes 10 to 12 scones***

**Banana Bread White Chocolate Scones**

# Banana Bread White Chocolate Scones

*These vanilla-glazed scones smell and taste like freshly baked banana bread but sport a delicate pastry pedigree. They irresistible and one of my personal favorites!*

## Scones

3 cups all-purpose flour
½ teaspoon baking soda
2 ½ teaspoons baking powder
3/8 teaspoon salt
1/8 teaspoon nutmeg
½ cup white sugar
1/3 cup brown sugar
¼ cup cream cheese
½ cup unsalted cold butter, in small cubes
1 egg
1 cup mashed banana
¾-1 cup whipping cream
1 teaspoon pure vanilla extract
½ cup white chocolate chips
½ cup chopped walnuts, optional

## Vanilla Bean Glaze

1 ½ cups confectioners' sugar
3 tablespoons unsalted butter, melted
1 tablespoon vanilla bean paste or
1 teaspoon pure vanilla extract

Preheat the oven to 400° F. Stack a large baking sheet on top of another one and line the top one with parchment paper. Arrange the oven rack to the middle or upper third position.

In a food processor blend the flour, baking soda, baking powder salt, nutmeg, white and brown sugar. Cut in cream cheese and butter to make a grainy mixture. Turn the mixture out into a large bowl. Make a well in the center and add the egg, banana, cream, and vanilla. Stir to make a stiff mixture and then add in the white chocolate and walnuts. If dough doesn't hold together, add a bit more cream. Turn out onto a lightly floured work surface and gentle pat into a round, about 10 inches in diameter. Cut in half, then in four and then cut each quadrant in two or three to make 8-12 scones. Bake until golden brown, about 15 minutes.

Meanwhile, for the Vanilla Bean Glaze, in a small bowl whisk together the confectioners' sugar, butter and vanilla bean paste or honey and vanilla extract. As scones cool, dip each one into the glaze to provide a thick coat and then let set.

***Makes 8-12 scones***

## Tollhouse Chocolate Chunk Scones

# Tollhouse Chocolate Chunk Scones

*A little brown sugar, some sweet butter and a hefty amount of chocolate chunks and you have a beautiful treat of a scone Tollhouse Cookie inventor, Mrs. Wakefield would be proud of.*

## Scones

¾ - 1 cup whipping cream
1 tablespoon lemon juice
3 cup all-purpose flour
1 cup brown sugar, firmly packed
1/2 cup white sugar
3/8 teaspoon salt
4 teaspoons baking powder
1/2 teaspoon baking soda
3/4 cup unsalted butter, in small cubes
1 egg
2 teaspoons pure vanilla extract
1 cup mixed semi-sweet chocolate and milk chocolate chunks or chips

## Finishing Touches

Melted butter
Brown sugar
Melted chocolate

In a measuring cup, mix the cream and lemon juice together and let stand a few minutes.

Preheat oven to 400° F. Stack two baking sheets together and line the top one with parchment paper. Arrange oven rack set to the upper third position.

In a food processor bowl, blend the flour, brown and white sugar, salt, baking powder and baking soda and blend briefly. Add in the butter and pulse to make a coarse, grainy mixture. Turn out into a large bowl. Make a well in the center and add in the cream, egg and vanilla and stir lightly with a fork to blend. Fold in the chocolate. If mixture is very wet, add a bit more flour (or a bit more plain cream if mixture seems too dry).

Turn out onto a lightly floured board and knead 8-10 times, until mixture is just barely rollable, again adding in a bit more flour to get a soft but manageable dough.

Pat or roll out 1 inch thick and cut into 6-inch circles. Then cut the circle in half, producing a rounded wedge. Brush tops with melted butter and bake until golden, about 12-15 minutes.

Allow scones to cool and then drizzle on melted chocolate, if you like.

**Makes 8-10 scones**

# Greek Yogurt Cherry Scones

# Greek Yogurt Cherry Scones

*Who can resist Greek yogurt with it its silky smooth texture! This recipe calls for thick-style Greek yogurt along with vibrant sour cherries and a touch of honey to sweeten the deal. If you don't have fresh sour cherries on hand, frozen or canned are fine. Slivered almonds on top are optional but heavenly.*

## Scones

3 cups all-purpose flour
2/3 cup sugar
2 tablespoons honey
½ teaspoon salt
1 tablespoon baking powder
½ teaspoon baking soda
½ cup unsalted butter, in small cubes
1 egg
1 cup Greek yogurt
½-1 cup milk or cream
1 cup pitted sour cherries, halved

## Finishing Touches

Melted butter
Honey

Preheat the oven to 400° F. Stack a large baking sheet on top of another one and line the top one with parchment paper. Arrange the oven rack to the middle or upper third position.

In a food processor, blend the flour, sugar, honey, salt, baking powder and baking soda. Pulse to blend. Then add in the butter and pulse to cut the butter into the dry ingredients. Turn the mixture out into a large bowl. Make a well in the center and add in the egg, yogurt and about 1/3 cup cream or milk and mix until almost blended. Fold in the cherries and mix to make soft scone dough, adding in more flour or liquid as required so that it holds together. Let rest 10 minutes.

Turn out onto a floured board and shape into a large round about one inch thick. Cut into wedges.

Place on baking sheet and bake until golden brown, 15-17 minutes. Brush with melted butter and warm honey as scones cool on baking sheet.

***Makes 8-12 scones***

# Multi Grain Scones

# Multi Grain Scones

*Scones are great carrier food as they adapt well to whatever you put into them. They're also great if you go the nutritious, grainy route. These are so satisfying! Although they're noble with the goodness of whole grains, they're still a delicate, sweet treat – just not decadent ones.*

## Scones

1 ½ cup unbleached all-purpose flour
¾ cup stoneground whole-wheat flour
½ cup kamut or spelt flour
¼ cup oatmeal
3/8 teaspoon salt
½ teaspoon baking soda
2 teaspoons baking powder
½ cup brown sugar packed
¼ cup maple syrup or honey
½ cup unsalted butter or cold coconut oil
1/3 cup mixed seeds: pumpkin, sesame, sunflower
1 tablespoon chai seeds
2 tablespoons flax seeds
¾ - 1 cup buttermilk
1 egg
1 cup plumped dried cranberries or cherries

## Finishing Touches

½ cup melted butter
1/3 cup honey

Preheat the oven to 400° F. Stack a large baking sheet on top of another one and line the top one with parchment paper. Arrange the oven rack to the middle or upper third position.

In a food processor, blend the white flour, whole-wheat flour, kamut, oatmeal, salt, baking soda, baking powder, brown sugar, and maple syrup or honey. Then add in the butter or coconut fat and pulse to cut the butter/coconut oil into the dry ingredients. Turn the mixture out into a large bowl and stir in the mixed seeds, chai seeds, flax seeds and mix briefly. Stir in the ¾ cup buttermilk and egg, mix to make a soft scone dough, adding in more buttermilk as required so that it holds together. Fold in the cranberries. Let stand 5 minutes. Turn out onto a lightly floured board and shape into a large round about one inch thick. Cut into wedges.

Place on baking sheet and bake until golden brown, 15-17 minutes.

Mix butter and honey together in a small bowl. Brush scones with the honey-butter mixture as they cool on the baking sheet.

***Makes 8-12 scones***

## Maple Walnut Scones

# Maple Walnut Scones

*These are rustic and satisfying and best of all, they're easy. These scones feature the best of rustic sweetness along with buttery walnuts and pure maple syrup.*

## Scones

3 cups all- purpose flour
1/3 cup brown sugar, firmly packed
4 teaspoons baking powder
3/4 teaspoon salt
1/4 teaspoon cinnamon
3/4 cup cold unsalted butter, cut in chunks
1/2 cup finely chopped walnuts
1 egg
1/3 cup pure maple syrup
1 teaspoon pure vanilla extract
3/4 -1 cup whipping cream

## Maple Fondant

1 1/2 cups confectioners' sugar
¼ cup pure maple syrup
¼ cup whipping cream
½ teaspoon pure vanilla extract
Finely chopped walnuts

Preheat the oven to 400° F. Stack a large baking sheet on top of another one and line the top one with parchment paper. Arrange the oven rack to the middle or upper third position.

In a food processor, blend the flour, brown sugar, baking powder, salt and cinnamon and pulse to combine ingredients. Add butter and pulse to break butter into flour mixture until you have a sandy mixture. Turn the mixture out into a large bowl and stir in walnuts. Make a well in the center and add the egg, maple syrup, vanilla and most of the cream. Stir with a fork to make a soft dough.

Turn out onto a lightly floured board and knead briefly. Add a bit more cream. If dough seems too dry; it should hold together. Shape the dough into a round, about 1 inch thick and 10 inches wide. Cut in half and then each half into 4-5 wedges each. Place them on the baking sheet.

Bake until browned, 18-22 minutes.

For the Maple Fondant, in a small bowl, blend the confectioners' sugar, maple syrup, cream, and vanilla to make a soft glaze. Smear over scones and then dust each scone with some finely chopped walnuts and let set.

***Makes 8-12 scones***

# Acknowledgements

**My warmest thanks to my volunteer recipe testers.
If each recipe is extra perfect, it is due to them**.

Cheryl Vockathaler, Recipe Tester and Editing

**Recipe Testers**
Louise Allen Louise Jacowitz Allen
Peggy Carroll-Tornberg
Yvonne Lachance
Deborah Racine

# Bonus Recipes with Purchase!

### Free 2-Months Access!
### Betterbaking.com

Please join me on this journey as we embark on another **Baker's Dozen Series Cookbook**. I wish you great success with each and every one of these special recipes. Don't forget my gift to you with your purchase! Just email me via www.Betterbaking.com with an electronic proof of your cookbook purchase to obtain your bonus two-month free subscription to Betterbaking.com Recipe Archives where you'll have all access to over 2500 more of my original recipes, online at my baking website and also receive my monthly newsletter with more free recipes.

# Other Books by Marcy Goldman

CPSIA information can be obtained
at www.ICGtesting.com
Printed in the USA
LVHW071559160122
708707LV00018B/722

9 781927 936405